RAILWAYS OF THE BRITISH EMPIRE

AUSTRALASIA AND BEYOND

COLIN ALEXANDER &
ALON SITON

AMBERLEY

First published 2022

Amberley Publishing
The Hill, Stroud
Gloucestershire, GL5 4EP

www.amberley-books.com

Copyright © Colin Alexander & Alon Siton, 2022

The right of Colin Alexander & Alon Siton to
be identified as the Authors of this work has
been asserted in accordance with the Copyrights,
Designs and Patents Act 1988.

ISBN 978 1 3981 0800 4 (print)
ISBN 978 1 3981 0801 1 (ebook)

British Library Cataloguing in Publication Data.
A catalogue record for this book is available from
the British Library.

Typesetting by SJmagic DESIGN SERVICES, India.
Printed in the UK.

INTRODUCTION

Everybody knows that Britannia ruled the waves, but it is perhaps less well known that she also ruled the rails. From the early nineteenth century Britain's engineers exported the Industrial Revolution, and especially the railway, across the world. This was especially true in those parts of the world that were coloured pink on schoolroom maps: the British Empire. The rapidly expanding colonial railways were supplied by British companies like Vulcan Foundry, Robert Stephenson, Neilson Reid, Bagnall, Kitson, Cravens and Cammell-Laird.

Long before the Portuguese built the first railways in Angola, the Belgians in the Congo and the French in Algeria, UK firms were exporting locomotives, rolling stock, signalling equipment, turntables, cranes and even bridges across the globe.

Future volumes in this series will look at British territories in the Indian subcontinent and Africa. This first volume is a nostalgic railway journey across the remainder of British Empire and beyond, evoking the days when Britain was the world's factory and her exports were shipped on British-built vessels, to countries as diverse as British Guyana, Canada and Australia.

Thousands of large items of equipment were transported by road or rail from Leeds, Manchester, Birmingham, Glasgow, Darlington and Newcastle-upon-Tyne to quaysides to be loaded upon cargo vessels for long voyages around the world. We can only marvel at the ingenuity of the earliest exporters, transferring locomotives from docksides to timber ships without hydraulic or steam cranes.

The export of British locomotives began in the late 1820s, before the Liverpool & Manchester Railway opened. These were to the United States and to Continental Europe.

What follows is a chronological summary of railway 'firsts' in the British Empire beyond the Indian subcontinent and Africa.

The first British overseas territory to reap the benefits of rail transport was, unsurprisingly, her nearest neighbour: Ireland. Less than ten years after the opening of George Stephenson's Stockton & Darlington Railway, 1834 saw the first trains between Dublin and Kingstown (later Dun Laoghaire) Harbour, intended to speed up the Royal Mail to and from Britain.

Across the Atlantic in 1836, the Champlain and St Lawrence Railroad was the first line in Canada, running 16 miles from the St Lawrence River at La Prairie to St Jean sur Richelieu on Lake Champlain. This connected two important navigable waterways and formed part of the trade route from Montreal to New York.

The first railway in Jamaica, which was also the first outside Europe and North America, opened in 1845. It connected the island's capital, Kingston, with Spanish Town, 13 miles distant. A network of over 200 miles eventually served most centres of population and there were also some private railways for the sugar cane industry.

Hundreds of miles to the south-east of Jamaica, the first railway on the entire South American continent was in British Guyana (now Guyana) in 1848. Opening of the Demerara Railway had been delayed when an inspection train struck a stray cow and derailed, resulting in two deaths.

Australia's railway age began in 1854 with the opening of a short line connecting Melbourne with Port Melbourne – at the time of the gold rush in Victoria. A year later the 14-mile line from Sydney to Parramatta began operation.

Across the Tasman Sea, the 5½-mile line from Christchurch to Ferrymead Wharf on the South Island was the first railway to operate in New Zealand, opening in 1863. It was a rare case of the permanent way being built to a gauge to suit the rolling stock, with second-hand vehicles coming from Australia.

Back in the Caribbean, as early as 1859 the island of Trinidad had a horse-drawn tram between Princes Town and San Fernando. Its first true railway opened in 1876, a 16-mile line from Port of Spain to the inland town of Arima. As was typical of the region, most of Trinidad's railways, which extended to 150 miles, were built for the sugar cane industry, but the last train ran in 1968.

The first section of the Barbados Railway was 8 miles long and opened in 1881, connecting the capital, Bridgetown, to Carrington. The engineering survey was carried out by Robert Fairlie, best known for his articulated locomotives.

As in the Caribbean, the railways of the Pacific island nation of Fiji were built for the movement of sugar cane. Steam haulage was in operation from 1882 on the earliest 2-foot-6-inch-gauge line. As almost 500 miles of railway spread across the two main islands of Viti Levu and Vanua Levu, most of it was built to the narrower gauge of 2 feet. In a rare example of social transportation, a free passenger service was provided on one of the main routes, but this ended in 1973.

A year after Fiji saw its first steam train, a 6½-mile metre-gauge railway opened on the Mediterranean island of Malta – from an underground terminus in the capital Valletta to Mdina. A short extension opened in 1900 to the military hospital at Mtarfa, but the railway closed in 1931.

The first railway in Malaya (now Malaysia) was the 7½-mile metre-gauge line from Taiping to Port Weld (Kuala Sepetang), which opened in 1885 to transport tin from the inland mines to the port. It was followed a year later by a 21-mile route connecting Kuala Lumpur with Klang, which was extended to Port Swettenham (Port Klang) by 1889. In 1901, the Federated Malay States Railway was established, uniting the country's various railways.

Separated from the southern tip of the Malay Peninsula by the Johore Strait (a narrow stretch of water that has gone by various names) is the island state of Singapore. The first steam railway there began operation in 1877, several years before that on the mainland. It would be 1903 before the Singapore to Kranji railway connected the island nation via ferry to mainland Malaya. In 1918 it became part of the Federated Malay States Railway (FMSR), and in 1923 a causeway was built to complete the physical rail link.

While the tiny British Overseas Territory of Gibraltar had a network of railways serving its docks, the station built to connect it to the rest of the European system was actually in Spain. This was the British-built Algeciras Gibraltar Railway, which ran to Bobadilla, north of Malaga, from Algeciras, across the Bay of Gibraltar from the eponymous Rock. It was engineered by Scotsman John Morrison and opened in 1890 to serve the British garrison.

Local newspaper *El Teléfono* said that the railway was 'purely and simply an extension of Gibraltar, constructed on behalf of the British government to augment Gibraltar's defensive powers in the Strait and convert it into a modern stronghold, using marbles and jaspers mined from Andalusian quarries'. It meant that the wives of British officers could escape the crowds and claustrophobia of The Rock for the beautiful Spanish countryside. Spanish folk benefited, too, for local peasant farmers could safely take their livestock and produce to market through a region previously notorious for bandits and rustlers.

At the opposite end of the Mediterranean Sea, the first railway in Palestine (then part of the Ottoman Empire) opened in 1892, a French-built metre-gauge route linking the port of Jaffa (now part of Tel-Aviv) to Jerusalem. Further north, in 1905 the Ottoman government built a 1,050-mm-gauge line through the Jezreel Valley from Haifa to Daraa (or Dera'a Junction) in Syria to carry materials needed for the construction of the Hedjaz Railway (the Pilgrims' Railway), with which it would eventually connect. The Hedjaz Railway headed south through the mountains of the same name, to the holy city of Medina in Arabia.

By the end of the First World War, the Ottoman Empire had been defeated and a British Mandate was declared on the territory between the River Jordan and the Mediterranean Sea. Despite repeated Turkish attacks, a trunk line was built by the British along the Mediterranean coast, stretching from Egypt to Haifa.

Once Palestine Railways took over operations from the British army in October 1920, it assumed responsibility for the rebuilt Jaffa–Jerusalem Railway, the Hedjaz Railway, the British-built line from Egypt to Haifa, and Tel-Aviv's suburban services. The network would become a target for terrorism in the years between the wars and what remained became the Israel State Railways in 1948.

The Caribbean island of Antigua had a 50-mile network of 2-foot-6-inch-gauge lines that served the sugar cane plantations. The first steam locomotives arrived from Britain in 1904.

A catastrophic drought in 1965 bankrupted the island's sugar industry, which was nationalised in 1967. In an attempt to diversify, a 5-mile section of the sugar cane line featured steam-hauled tourist trains under the name of 'Sunshine Choo-Choo' from 1968 until 1973.

Yet another island nation of the Empire, Cyprus in the eastern Mediterranean saw the opening of the 2-foot-6-inch-gauge Cyprus Government Railway in 1905. This first section ran 37 miles from the main port, Famagusta, to the capital, Nicosia. By 1915 extensions to Morphou and Evrykhou doubled the route mileage, but the first closures took place in 1932. The original 1905 section was last to close – in 1951.

Jordan became a British protectorate in 1921, by which time the aforementioned Hedjaz Railway had been in operation for thirteen years. It passed through Jordan on its way from Damascus in Syria to Medina in what is now Saudi Arabia. During the time of the British mandate, a number of UK-built locomotives were supplied.

In complete contrast from the deserts of Jordan we head for the southern Atlantic outpost of South Georgia, a most unlikely location for railway activity. This inhospitable and remote island saw the establishment of several whaling stations, one of which, A/S Ocean, used a narrow-gauge railway. It was operational from 1909 but by 1920 was out of use. Remarkably, some relics remain, including a shipwreck and a steam locomotive.

The British territory of Hong Kong was served by tramways from 1888, but it was not until the arrival of the Canton Kowloon Railway in 1910 that proper trains were seen. The Public Works Department of the Hong Kong government began construction on the section between Tai Po Market and Fan Ling in December 1905.

The first railway on the Caribbean island of St Kitts was another 2-foot-6-inch-gauge system for the carrying of sugar cane. It opened in 1912 and was extended to serve more plantations, but by the 1990s most of it was out of use. Happily, in 2003, an 18-mile section on the east coast was reopened from La Valle to Basseterre as a tourist attraction.

Iraq's first line was built to standard gauge and opened in 1914, connecting Baghdad with the ancient city of Samarra, 75 miles to the north. This was part of the grand Ottoman Baghdad Railway scheme to link Iraq with Istanbul and mainland Europe. Six years later the British mandate in Iraq began, and railways began to spread to the main areas of population, especially in the valleys of Mesopotamia, now using metre-gauge track.

The island nation of Bermuda has no railways today, but it is possible to walk along several sections of the former 26-mile standard-gauge line. This opened in 1931 along the length of the island chain from Somerset to St George, and closed in 1948.

There were minor railways scattered across several other British overseas territories. They included the Bahamas, British Honduras (now Belize), British New Guinea (Papua Territory), Dominica, Nauru, Saint Lucia and East Caicos in the Turks and Caicos Islands. Most of these were built for the transport of sugar cane, or other crops or minerals for export; or, in the case of the Falkland Islands, for strategic purposes to serve a radio transmitter.

As well as the railways in the Empire itself, there were other countries in which railways were built and operated by British companies, most notably in Brazil and Argentina.

Finally, being at the forefront of railway development meant that many countries naturally turned to British engineers to supply locomotives. This led to the appearance of British-built machines all over Europe, the USA, Russia, Japan and even China. There is one other British railway export that can be seen far and wide, and that is George Stephenson's standard gauge, in which the rails are laid 4 feet 8½ inches apart, just as they were at Killingworth Colliery in Northumberland where his first locomotive ran in 1814.

Lamentably, in the twenty-first century the situation is reversed. Whereas British companies once operated railways in South America, the UK's rail franchises now make profits for nationalised rail networks overseas. Where Britain was once the workshop to the world, trains built here now are based on Japanese technology and we rely on imported motive power from North America and Continental Europe. It is a sad state of affairs for the country that so proudly invented the railway and supplied the world.

The following images will take us around the territories of the Empire, apart from India and Africa, in a geographical sequence, heading south and east from Ireland around the globe, and finishing in the South Atlantic. Then follows a selection of British-built locomotives for export elsewhere. This book would not have been possible without Alon Siton, the driving force and inspiration behind it, and whose extensive photographic collection forms its basis. Thanks also to Greg Martin and Helmut Dahlhaus for their invaluable assistance, and the other individual photographers who have kindly contributed, including the wonderful archive of ETH Zürich.

This image comes from the 1923 catalogue of Kitson's, Leeds. All of the major locomotive manufacturers showcased their products in glossy publications to attract lucrative contracts from both home and abroad. This view of the erecting shop depicts 2-6-0s for England's Great Northern Railway under construction, but it also shows the multiple rails to accommodate a variety of track gauges for export orders. (Alon Siton collection)

The Dublin & Kingstown Railway was Ireland's first passenger line and the inaugural train was hauled by 2-2-0 *Hibernia*, built at Sharp, Roberts in Manchester, in 1834. Three locomotives of that wheel arrangement were also supplied the same year by the Liverpool firm of George Forrester, including *Vauxhall*, seen here. Much of the line remains in use as part of the DART rapid transit system. (Alon Siton collection)

The 30-mile Cork & Youghal Railway was originally part of a scheme to connect Cork to the Great Western Railway via Waterford and a ferry connection, but Youghal was as far as it ever got. Isambard Kingdom Brunel, who was keen to establish a link between the GWR and Ireland, was its engineer. He died before completion in 1859. 2-4-0ST No. 5 *Pike* was built by Neilson of Glasgow in 1860. (Alon Siton collection)

Whereas the Cork & Youghal was built to the Irish broad gauge of 5 feet 3 inches, the Cavan & Leitrim Railway in the north-west of Ireland was laid to a 3-foot gauge. It employed eight 4-4-0T locomotives such as No. 5 *Gertrude*, built by Robert Stephenson's in Newcastle-upon-Tyne in 1887, the year of the railway's opening. Sister engine *Kathleen* is preserved in the Ulster Folk & Transport Museum at Cultra. (Alon Siton collection)

Another broad-gauge line was the Dublin, Wicklow & Wexford Railway. This handsome 4-4-2T, No. 54, was supplied by Sharp Stewart in 1892. The railway absorbed the aforementioned Dublin & Kingstown and became the Dublin & South Eastern Railway in 1906. Sharp Stewart, along with fellow Glaswegian firms Dübs and Neilson Reid, would merge in 1903 to form the giant North British Locomotive Company, the largest outside the USA. (Alon Siton collection)

The first ceremonial sod in the construction of the West Clare Railway was cut by formidable Irish nationalist politician Charles Stewart Parnell. It was a narrow-gauge line connecting Ennis to Kilrush, and the first section opened in 1887. In 1948, Irish National Railways (CIE) replaced steam with diesel traction and it continued in operation until 1961. 2-6-2T No. 8 *Lisdoonvarna* was built by Dübs in 1894. (Alon Siton collection)

The Manchester firm of Beyer Peacock received many locomotive orders from Irish railways. The Belfast & County Down Railway covered the territory to the east and south of Belfast, as far as Newcastle. It purchased several of these neat 0-6-0s, the first of which was built at Beyer Peacock's Gorton Foundry in 1904. She lasted in service for fifty years. (Alon Siton collection)

The following year, the same locomotive builder supplied the Dublin, Wicklow & Wexford Railway with this handsome 0-6-0, No. 66 *Dublin*. Note the elegant way in which her nameplate is incorporated into the splasher over the centre drivers. She was built by Beyer Peacock in 1905. (Alon Siton collection)

In the far north-west of Ireland lay the Londonderry & Lough Swilly Railway, which built the Letterkenny & Burtonport Extension Railway in 1903, heading west into County Donegal towards the Atlantic Ocean. Compared to some of the locomotives we have seen so far, this one is a giant. L&BER 4-8-4T No. 5, and sister No. 6, were built by Hudswell Clarke of Leeds in 1912. (Alon Siton collection)

Ireland's railways continued to order locomotives from British manufacturers long after the Irish Free State was created in 1922, although by this time Ireland was building her own locomotives, too. The Great Northern Railway of Ireland ordered the five members of its Class VS 4-4-0 from Beyer Peacock in 1948. They were named after rivers, such as No. 208 *Lagan*, seen here in workshop primer outside the Gorton Foundry. They are believed to have been the last 4-4-0s to be built anywhere. (Alon Siton collection)

Due south from Dublin, we find another handsome Beyer Peacock 4-4-0, featuring the company name cast into her brass splasher ornamentation. No. 8 *Castellar* was built in Manchester in 1912 for the Ferrocarril Algeciras-Bobadilla. This was the British-built railway serving the military outpost of Gibraltar. The line later became part of the Ferrocarriles Andaluces and eventually RENFE. (Alon Siton collection)

Further into the Mediterranean, the Malta Railway ran from the capital, Valletta to Mtarfa, and was in operation from 1883 until 1931. Competition from electric trams in the early twentieth century had a major effect on its profitability, compounded when motor buses were introduced in 1905. This view shows the charming Museum Station at Mtarfa with the impressive barracks in the distance. (ETH Zürich)

A total of ten steam locomotives were supplied to the Malta Railway by Manning Wardle of Leeds, Black Hawthorn of Gateshead and Beyer Peacock of Manchester. The latter supplied four 2-6-4T engines, Nos 7–10, one of which is seen heading a train in Valletta in 1918. (Jordan Gauci, Bay Retro Archive)

Unusually, the Maltese capital, Valletta, had an underground station beneath the Floriana, obscured in the previous image by the train. This view shows the entrance to the tunnel beneath the fortified headland at St Philip's Gardens. Trains carried ammunition from the magazine here to the barracks at Mtarfa as part of the island's defence system, and during the Second World War, the disused tunnel saw use as an air-raid shelter. (Colin Alexander collection)

Locomotive No. 1 of the 2-foot-6-inch-gauge Cyprus Railway was an 0-6-0T built by Hunslet of Leeds in 1904. She is preserved today on a plinth in Famagusta, as seen here. The only other steam locomotives that survive on the island are two derelict American-built tank engines from the Cyprus Mines Corporation. (Wayne Hopkins, Texas, USA)

As the Cyprus Railway grew in route mileage it needed extra locomotives. Kitson's of Leeds built two 4-8-4Ts in 1915, to be joined by another pair in 1920. They were numbered 41–44, and the first of them is seen here in steam at Famagusta. The railway played a significant part in moving troops and ammunition during the Second World War, but closed in 1951. (Alon Siton collection)

If those troops sailed south-east from Cyprus they would have landed in Palestine. This historic image shows a British military train of clerestory coaches headed by London & South Western Railway 0-6-0 No. 28, built by Neilson in 1885. She was one of many British locomotives to see overseas wartime service, and was employed by Palestine Military Railways during the First World War. The location is Jerusalem, shortly after the British takeover from the Ottoman army. (Israel Railways Museum, Haifa)

Birmingham Railway Carriage & Wagon was founded in the 1850s and enjoyed an international reputation for its vehicles. This is the sumptuous interior of Palestine Railways saloon No. 98, built by BRC&W in 1922 and now preserved at the Israel Railways Museum, Haifa. Her famous passengers have included Emperor Haile Selassie of Ethiopia, and Sir Winston Churchill. (Alon Siton collection)

For the steep climb from Jaffa to Jerusalem, Palestine Railways obtained six new 2-8-4T locomotives from Kitson of Leeds in 1922. They were designated Class K, with 4-foot-diameter drivers to cope with heavy traffic, but were prone to derailment. This 1930s portrait taken at Jerusalem station shows a small crowd, perhaps of railway employees, gathered in front of one of them. (Alon Siton collection)

Kantara East was where Palestine Railways' British-built Haifa to Cairo railway line crossed the Suez Canal, on its way across the Sinai desert. It was the location for this undated scene, showing a Class N locomotive of Palestine Railways. Ten of these outside-cylindered 0-6-0T shunting engines were built from 1934 by Nasmyth Wilson of Manchester. (Alon Siton collection)

Palestine Railways ordered six of these handsome P Class 4-6-0 mixed-traffic locomotives from North British in 1935. This official portrait shows the first, No. 60, upon completion in Glasgow. Following the end of the British Mandate in 1947 they became Israel State Railway motive power. They lasted in service until 1960, but sadly only two of the tenders survive in preservation. (Alon Siton collection)

The War Department ordered 240 Stanier 8F 2-8-0s for use overseas during the Second World War, and many remained abroad in peacetime. This is Israel State Railways No. 70400, built by Beyer Peacock in Manchester in 1940. She served in Iran and with the Middle East Forces, lasting in service until 1958. She is seen here in Beirut, with superficial damage to cylinder cladding and cowcatcher, having struck a van carrying Indian military personnel at an unmanned level crossing at Chekka, in western Lebanon. (Alon Siton collection)

During the Second World War, Allied forces built a railway along the Mediterranean coast from Haifa into Lebanon, intended to connect Europe via Turkey to North Africa. The Haifa, Beirut & Tripoli Railway tunnelled through the chalk cliffs at Rosh Hanikra, as seen in this 1959 view. By this time the 1942-built line was abandoned due to the political situation in the region, and later a road was built on much of its trackbed. Note the 'beware – border!' sign in Hebrew at the end of the severed track in the tunnel entrance. (Alon Siton collection)

Although the British were less involved in the development of Jordan's railways than elsewhere, several British-built locomotives were employed there. This 4-6-4T, built by North British in 1941, was one of six originally built for the metre-gauge Federated Malay States Railway. The Japanese occupation of Malaya saw them instead being commandeered by the Ministry of Supply for use in Egypt, and they were handed to the Hedjaz Railway in 1951. (Alon Siton collection)

This is the Hedjaz Railway station at Amman, capital of Jordan, in 1980, and 2-8-2 No. 23 is seen under a cloudless blue sky. She was the third of three 'Mikados' built by Robert Stephenson & Hawthorns in 1952, and two are believed to survive in preservation. (Alon Siton collection)

These metre-gauge 4-6-0s double-heading a freight train in 1967 were built several years before Iraq's first railway was built. Iraqi State Railways' No. 107 was built by Vulcan Foundry in 1910 and No. 144 by Nasmyth Wilson in 1909. An example of railways acquiring second-hand equipment from elsewhere in the Empire, they came from the East Bengal Railway and the Madras & Southern Mahratta Railway, respectively. (Alon Siton collection)

Several British companies specialised in rolling stock, as opposed to locomotives. One such was Gloucester Railway Carriage & Wagon. This image, taken around the time of the First World War, shows an Iraq Railway postal coach under construction. It is possible that the bodywork of such vehicles was shipped 'flat-packed', to be assembled on arrival. (Alon Siton collection)

In 1923, the Sentinel Waggon Works of Shrewsbury, an established manufacturer of geared steam road vehicles, diversified into rail traction. This was in collaboration with Cammell, Laird of Nottingham, with whom several steam railcars were built for railways around the world. They included this 1927 example for Iraq. (Alon Siton collection)

The glamorous streamliners of the 1930s captured European and American imaginations. Not to be outdone, the Iraqi State Railway ordered four streamlined Pacifics from Robert Stephenson & Hawthorn's of Darlington, including No. 502 *Mosul*, seen here in an official works portrait. The PC Class 4-6-2s were built in 1940, with styling clearly influenced by Gresley's A4s and Stanier's Coronations. (Alon Siton collection)

Perhaps even more striking than the PCs' profile was the sculpted rear of the tender. They were ordered for the haulage of express trains on the newly completed route from Baghdad to Istanbul. Named after Iraqi cities, one of the quartet, No. 504 *Kirkuk* was lost at sea en route to Iraq from England. (Alon Siton collection)

The Iraqi State Railway owned at least three British-built steam cranes. The largest was of 75-ton capacity, ordered from Ransomes & Rapier of Ipswich. This 1988 photograph taken at Baghdad East shows one of the smaller ones, a 25-ton crane built by Cowans Sheldon in Carlisle, which entered service in 1948. (Alon Siton collection)

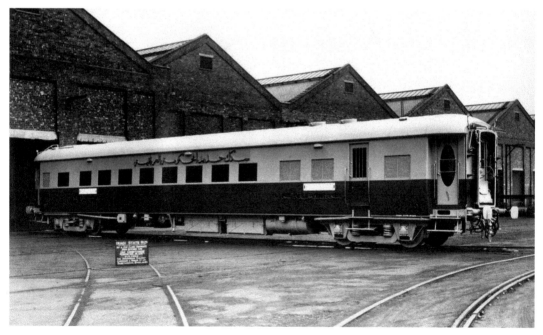

Compare the timber-bodied postal coach above to this stylish Iraqi State Railways carriage of the early 1950s. It combined air-conditioned, first- and second-class accommodation with kitchen facilities, and was built by Birmingham Railway Carriage & Wagon. The oval window in the vestibule doors is a nod to Pullman car styling. (Alon Siton collection)

Earlier, we saw the massive Irish 4-8-4T built by Hudswell Clarke, a manufacturer known mostly for smaller British industrial locomotives. They also built this modern metre-gauge 2-8-4T, one of three for the Iraq Petroleum Company. Like much of the Middle East, by the beginning of the twenty-first century, Iraq's rail network was run down and greatly damaged by the Gulf Wars. Despite this, much of the system remains, including the original Baghdad Railway to Turkey via Syria. (Alon Siton collection)

Continuing our eastward exploration of former British territories we bypass the Indian subcontinent, covered in the first volume, and arrive at the colonial outpost of Hong Kong. Several British-built locomotives arrived for the opening of the Canton Kowloon Railway including a number of 2-6-0s built by North British, such as this one of 1909. The same firm also supplied similar machines for mainland China. (ETH Zürich)

At least one of these Canton Kowloon Railway 2-6-0s was redeployed by the British at the other end of Asia, on the Haifa, Beirut & Tripoli Railway. No. 70219, another 1909 North British-built locomotive, ended her days in Beirut, as seen here, where she was used for shunting duties. (Alon Siton collection)

Contemporary with the 2-6-0s was a class of eight inside-cylinder 2-6-4T engines, built by Kitson in Leeds, becoming CKR Nos 1–8. Like the Moguls, most of them were commandeered by the War Department during the Second World War and shipped west, becoming part of the Middle East Forces stable of locomotives. (Alon Siton collection)

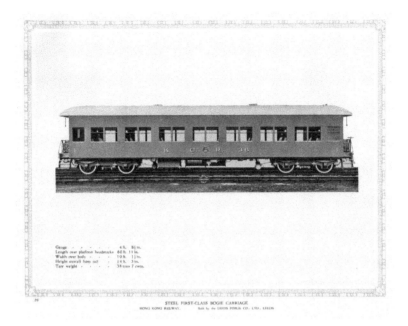

STEEL FIRST-CLASS BOGIE CARRIAGE
HONG KONG RAILWAY.   Built by the LEEDS FORGE CO., LTD., LEEDS

Construction work in Hong Kong was slow due to labour shortages, malaria, beriberi and dysentery, and the difficulties of excavating Beacon Hill Tunnel. The first section opened on 1 October 1910 and a year later the mainland Chinese section to Canton (now Guangzhou) was completed. Operation began five days before the start of the 1911 Revolution that led to the abdication of the last Qing emperor in 1912. This page from a Cammell Laird catalogue, possibly from the 1920s, shows a steel first-class carriage for the Hong Kong Railway, built in Leeds. (Alon Siton collection)

Exemplifying Britain's influence in her far-flung territories is the frontage of Hong Kong's Kowloon terminus decorated for the coronation of Elizabeth II in 1953. The station opened in 1916 but, owing to lack of space for expansion, was replaced in 1974. The Hong Kong Cultural Centre stands on this site today. Note the very British-looking bus and saloon car, both driving on the left. (Colin Alexander collection)

One of the first locomotives in Malaya was this Selangor Government Railway 4-4-0T from Neilson of Glasgow in 1888. She joined three similar locomotives that had arrived from Hunslet of Leeds for the opening of the line in 1886. They were used on passenger trains and were given names such as *Lady Clementi* and *Lady Mitchell*, which led to the line being nicknamed 'the Aristocrats Line'. (ETH Zürich)

This charming third-class coach, built in 1893 for the Selangor Government Railway, would have been hauled by those 'aristocratic' 4-4-0Ts. It was a product of Gloucester Railway Carriage & Wagon. (Alon Siton collection)

Formed in 1901, the Federated Malay States Railway strengthened the locomotive fleet inherited from its constituents, such as the aforementioned Selangor Railway, with a total of thirty-four of these Class G 4-6-0s. They were built by Hunslet, Robert Stephenson's and Neilson, with the majority, including No. 57 seen here, by Kitson of Leeds. The last two were withdrawn in July 1947. (Julian Rainbow)

There is more than a passing family resemblance between the Class Gs 4-6-0 seen above and this FMSR Class L 4-6-2, No. 214, which emerged from Kitson's twenty years later, in 1921. Later becoming No. 531.01, she is preserved at the National Museum in Kuala Lumpur. (Alon Siton collection)

Unusually for a main-line company, the FMSR built a funicular railway, the first in South East Asia. This was the Penang Hills Railway, which opened to the public in 1924, engineered by Arnold Robert Johnson and using Swiss technology. Until 2010, it operated in two sections with a midway changeover point, then it was rebuilt and modernised as a continuous run. (ETH Zürich)

With her large boiler and high running plate, this three-cylinder 4-6-2 built for the FMSR by North British looks altogether more modern than the earlier Kitson Pacific. She was one of a 1928 trio built in Glasgow and, despite being metre-gauge engines with 4-foot-6-inch-diameter driving wheels, they were capable of 70 mph. (Alon Siton collection)

Above: In 1962, FMSR became Keretapi Tanah Melayu Berhad (Malaysia Railways), usually abbreviated to KTM. Among the locomotives absorbed by the renamed company was this Class K2 4-6-2, No. 542.02, formerly FMSR No.152. She was one of four built by Robert Stephenson's in Darlington in 1929, and they lasted in service into the 1970s. (Alon Siton collection)

Right: As with most of the colonial railways scattered across the Empire, the FMSR realised there was a potential among intrepid Europeans for tourist traffic. This beautiful 1933 poster advertises 'The Golden Chersonese', a service whose name derived from the ancient Greek and Latin for the Malay Peninsula, as referred to by Ptolemy in his *Geographia*. (Alon Siton collection)

WAGON STOCK

BOGIE CATTLE WAGON FOR MALAYAN RAILWAYS

Interior view showing water troughs and centre partition

Length over buffers ... ... 42 ft. 9¼ ins.	Max. width inside body ... 8 ft. 5 ins.
Length over headstocks ... 39 ft. 0 ins.	Height inside at centres ... 7ft. 10¾ ins.
Length over body ... ... 38 ft. 9¾ ins.	Centres of bogies ... ... 27 ft. 0 ins.

Metre Gauge
Tare Weight :—16 tons 5 cwts.

View of underside of welded underframe

CRAVENS · SHEFFIELD · ENGLAND

42

From the glamour of named expresses to the everyday business of transporting livestock. Not only did the state railways advertise to travellers; similarly, the manufacturers advertised their wares to the railway companies. This page from a 1950s catalogue produced by Cravens of Sheffield shows a bogie cattle wagon built for service in Malaya. (Alon Siton collection)

The end of the turmoil of the Second World War in South East Asia did not signal an end to British imports; in fact, many of the world's railways were in a desperate need to re-equip. This modern, pressure-ventilated composite night coach was built in 1954 by Birmingham Railway Carriage & Wagon. (Alon Siton collection)

As the world's post-war railways modernised, Vulcan Foundry of Newton-le-Willows was at the forefront of diesel and electric traction for home and abroad, under the name of English Electric. The twenty-six members of Class 20, a 1,500-hp Co-Co design, were the first main-line diesel locomotives in Malaya, introduced in 1957. Numbered 20101–26, they immediately took over principal expresses and were equally at home on freight. One example has been preserved. (Melanie Dennis)

Singapore Kranji Railway, Singapore.

Off the southern tip of the Malay Peninsula lies the independent island of Singapore. In 1903, Kranji, on the north side of the island, was linked by rail to the capital and by ferry to the mainland. Somewhere along that route is the location for this image printed on a vintage postcard. In 2016, Singapore and Malaysia agreed to the construction of a high-speed rail link connecting the two countries. Expected to open by 2026, the journey time from Kuala Lumpur to Singapore will be cut to 90 minutes. (ETH Zürich)

We now leave Asia behind, and a year after Australia's first steam-hauled passenger train left Melbourne, the first to run in New South Wales was hauled by 0-4-2 No. 1, designed by James McConnell. She was built in Newcastle-upon-Tyne in 1854 by Robert Stephenson, that firm's 958th locomotive. She is now proudly displayed in the Powerhouse Museum in Sydney. (Bill Johnston)

The Thirlmere Railway Precinct is a major railway museum in New South Wales. Among its many British-built exhibits is Z(13) Class 4-4-2T No. 1301, built in 1877 by Beyer Peacock. She features that company's distinctive sloping running plate over her inclined cylinders, and has many similarities with the famous Metropolitan Railway 4-4-0Ts. She was originally a C(79) Class 4-4-0 tender locomotive, and was converted in Australia to a tank engine for suburban services around Sydney. (Kevin Bradney)

Another Thirlmere resident built by Beyer Peacock in 1877 is A(93) Class 0-6-0 No. 1905. She was originally No. 97, one of a class of seventy-seven from various builders for freight work. With their characteristic cab-side portholes, they were the final New South Wales Government Railway development of the 'long-boiler' 0-6-0. No. 1905's claim to fame is that she was the first locomotive to cross the Sydney Harbour Bridge. (Kevin Bradney)

Also a product of Beyer Peacock, this vertical-boilered steam tram locomotive was built in 1885 and sent to Sydney's New South Wales Government Tramways for comparison against an American Baldwin engine. The Baldwin was more successful, so the British engine was sent home, but not before she was used on colliery and construction jobs. She returned to Beyer Peacock and became a works shunter at Gorton Foundry, and is preserved at Crich Tramway Village in Derbyshire. (Alon Siton collection)

One of the world's most remarkable preservation survivors is No. 1 *The Major*. Nine of these 0-6-4T locomotives were built by Beyer Peacock in 1885 for the Mersey Railway, with its gradients of 1 in 27 in the tunnel between Liverpool and Birkenhead. They had what were then the largest cylinders on a British locomotive. When the line was electrified, four of the engines were sold for colliery work in Australia, and No. 1 survives at Thirlmere. Sister locomotive No. 5 *Cecil Raikes* is in the Museum of Liverpool. (Trent Nicholson)

Yet another Beyer Peacock product, the Australian standard 2-6-0 was built from 1885, and was seen in several territories. Twenty-seven were supplied to Tasmania for goods work, and a twenty-eighth was acquired second-hand, being designated Class C. The Tasmanian Transport Museum at Glenorchy is the setting for this charming 1994 scene, with a very British-looking signal box and lattice semaphore signal posts. No. C22 dates from 1902 and is the most original of the preserved Cs, retaining her sloping smokebox front. (Melanie Dennis)

Six members of the C Class were modified with larger cylinders and boiler, and reclassified as CCS. Tasmanian Government Railways CCS No. 23 was the last steam locomotive in service on the island and survives in preservation, having starred in the TGR's centenary celebrations of 1971. She is seen here on the Don River Railway in 1977. (Melanie Dennis)

This is the first of twelve handsome 4-4-0s built at Vulcan Foundry in 1886, becoming NSWGR Class Z(17). They originally carried the numbers 373–84, and the last was withdrawn from service in 1957. No. 381, later No. 1709, was returned to steam to operate 'specials' for a time, but she is now retired and is another Thirlmere exhibit. (Alon Siton collection)

Due to Australia's size and the isolated nature of her developing railways, at least sixteen different track gauges were used across her seven territories. By 1917, a journey on the new Transcontinental Railway required eight changes of gauge between Perth and Brisbane. Compare the standard-gauge 4-4-0 in the previous image with No. 170, a 3-foot-6-inch-gauge locomotive of the same wheel arrangement built by Kitson in 1888 for Western Australia's Great Southern Railway. (Alon Siton collection)

With track laid to the same 3-foot-6-inch gauge, the beautifully named Emu Bay and Mount Bischoff Railway on the west coast of Tasmania was originally a horse-worked wooden tramway. Its purpose was to transport tin ore to the coast at Burnie. EB&MBR locomotive No. 3 was an 0-6-4T built by Neilson's in Glasgow in 1888. (ETH Zürich)

The architecture of Britain's grandest Victorian stations was emulated in the principal cities of the Empire. Opened in 1889, Queensland Government Railways' Brisbane Central station was built of timber and corrugated iron. Ten years later it was replaced by this permanent and altogether more magnificent building. The landmark clock tower and portico were designed by architect J. J. Clark. (ETH Zürich)

In 1891, New South Wales Government Railways began taking delivery of fifteen Class M(40) 4-4-2T locomotives from Beyer Peacock in Manchester. They were built for the expanding suburban network and were described by the great O. S. Nock as excellent engines. They lasted in service until the 1920s when, with traffic growing ever heavier, they were replaced by more powerful machines. (Alon Siton collection)

The Eastern Goldfields Railway was built by Western Australian Government Railways to link the gold mines at Coolgardie and Kalgoorlie with Perth. Neilson of Glasgow supplied twenty-four locomotives of K Class 2-8-4T to work the line and they were the most powerful locos in Western Australia at the time. Another six were ordered by the British War Office for use in the Boer War in South Africa. This example, No. 104, was built in 1893. (ETH Zürich)

Even when an Australian locomotive builder constructed locomotives to an American design, there was still an element of British influence. This is the only time I have ever seen a photo of a classic American 4-4-0 with conventional buffers and a very British chimney. She is Queensland Government Railways' Class A14 4-4-0 steam locomotive No. 282, built by the Phoenix Engine Company, Ipswich, Queensland in 1894. (Alon Siton collection)

Western Australian Government Railways' Class O 2-8-0 was designed as a lighter version of the aforementioned K Class 2-8-4T, and, like the tank engines, they were built by Neilson's. This official portrait shows No. 74, built in 1896. Note the additional water tank in front of the cab. Sister engine No. 218 is preserved in the Rail Heritage WA museum at Bassendean. (ETH Zürich)

ROBERT STEPHENSON & CO., Ltd.   DARLINGTON

Type 4-4-4 Tank Locomotive for Suburban Traffic, Western Australian Government Railways.
Locomotive-Tender à 2 essieux accouplés pour les Chemins de Fer de l'Etat Ouest-Australien.
2/6 gek. Tender-Lokomotive für Vorortverkehr für die W. Australischen Regierungseisenbahnen.
Locomotora de 2 ejes acoplados para los Ferrocarriles del Gobierno de Oeste-Australia.
—4—

Robert Stephenson's 1910 catalogue illustrates this Class N suburban passenger 4-4-4T for the Western Australian Government Railways. Twelve of these were built at Forth Street works in Newcastle-upon-Tyne in 1898 and one, No. 201, is preserved at Bassendean. (Alon Siton collection)

With the combination pannier-and-side tanks that were a hallmark of Kitson tank engines, this is Western Australian Government Railways' Class B 4-6-0T No. 182, built in Leeds in 1898. She is coupled to a bolster wagon while engaged in shunting at Fremantle, circa 1926. Note the smartly attired shunter, nonchalantly perched on the cab footsteps. (Alon Siton collection)

Also in 1898, on the other side of Australia, New South Wales Government Railways took delivery of a batch of ten 2-8-0 locomotives from Neilson's. They were part of the 50 Class of standard goods engine, which eventually totalled 280 locomotives. No. 548 was built in Glasgow and entered service in October 1898, lasting in service until 1956. (Alon Siton collection)

The Canning Jarrah Timber Company of Western Australia provided much of the timber required to build the growing railway network. This 2-6-2TT locomotive, an 1899 product of Kitson's, Leeds, was named *J H Smith* and was used to haul trainloads of logs. She is seen with her crew posing on the side tank and buffer beam. The locomotive was scrapped in 1958. (Alon Siton collection)

One of the few British locomotive builders not based in the northern half of the country was Avonside of Bristol. Tasmania's North Mount Lyell Railway purchased three neat 4-6-0 locomotives from that firm in 1899. The middle one of the trio, No.2 *J. P. Lonergan* is seen here in an official workshop portrait. They were designed by David Jones of the Highland Railway, and share some features with his famous goods engine, which was Britain's first 4-6-0. He also designed 4-8-0s for the nearby Emu Bay Railway. (ETH Zürich)

Western Australia's E Class 4-6-2s were built by Vulcan Foundry, North British and Nasmyth Wilson from 1902. They were among the first Pacifics built in Britain, and for twenty years were the mainstay of passenger motive power in the territory. No. 348, seen here, was built in Glasgow by North British in 1911. Vulcan-built sister No. 308 is preserved at Bassendean. (Alon Siton collection)

Visually similar to the E Class 4-6-2, and also introduced in 1902, WAGR's Class F 4-8-0 was designed for heavy freight haulage. The first batch came from Dübs in Glasgow, and its successor North British built the remainder, including No. 365 seen here, which entered service in 1912 and lasted fifty-eight years. Two are preserved. (Alon Siton collection)

No. 3001 was built by Beyer Peacock in 1903 as a 4-6-4T, the first of 145 Class C30 locomotives for Sydney suburban services. When electrification arrived, seventy-seven were converted to 4-6-0 tender engines for use on rural branch lines. Finally withdrawn in the early 1970s, she was handed over to the NSW Rail Museum, and from 1983 she was used on mainline rail tours. Today, she is a static exhibit at Thirlmere. (Kevin Bradney)

Several British railway companies operated steam railmotors, consisting of a small locomotive articulated to a passenger coach. Others were built for export, such as this 1906 example for South Australian Railways, nicknamed the 'Coffee Pot'. The locomotive section was built by Kitson, and the coach by Metropolitan of Birmingham. She was restored to working order in 1984 at the Pichi Richi Railway and is the only survivor operating anywhere in the world. (Caleb's Rail Films)

The locomotive type that would conquer much of the world evolved from this little engine. 1909 saw the emergence of the first Beyer Garratt, North East Dundas Tramway 0-4-0+0-4-0 No. 1, built by Beyer Peacock. Later becoming K1 of the Tasmanian Government Railways, this handsome machine later returned to the UK, where she was returned to full working order and used on the spectacular Welsh Highland Railway. (Alon Siton collection)

J & A Brown's Richmond Vale Railway served four collieries in New South Wales. Its locomotive fleet included three 2-8-2Ts built by Kitson, the middle one of which was No. 10 *Richmond Main*, built in Leeds in 1911. She is seen here at Hexham yard in 1972. They were essentially tank engine versions of Robinson's 8-coupled Great Central Railway tender locos. No. 10 remained in use until 1976 and is preserved at Richmond Main. (Alon Siton collection)

For its Perth suburban services, the WAGR ordered twenty 4-6-4Ts from North British. Known as the D Class, they were the tank locomotive equivalent of the E Class. Phased out by dieselisation from the 1950s, the last was withdrawn in 1965. No. 385, pictured here, was built in 1912. (Alon Siton collection)

Kitson's of Leeds was very productive in the period immediately before The First World War. In 1912 they built five lightweight 4-6-2s for the Midland Railway of Western Australia. No. 18, previously numbered 15, is seen here in 1960 with a Railway Historical Society rail tour at Midland Junction, on the north-eastern edge of Perth. Sadly, despite several such outings, she was scrapped in 1963. (Alon Siton collection)

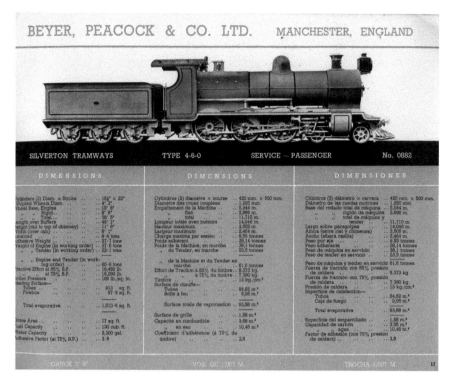

BEYER, PEACOCK & CO. LTD.   MANCHESTER, ENGLAND

| SILVERTON TRAMWAYS | TYPE 4-6-0 | SERVICE — PASSENGER | No. 0882 |

DIMENSIONS			DIMENSIONS			DIMENSIONES		
Cylinders (2) Diam. x Stroke		16¼" × 22"	Cylindres (2) diamètre × course		420 mm. × 560 mm.	Cilindros (2) diámetro × carrera		420 mm. × 560 mm.
Coupled Wheels Diam.		4' 3"	Diamètre des roues couplées		1.295 mm.	Diámetro de las ruedas motrices		1.295 mm.
Wheel Base, Engine		19' 6"	Empattement de la Machine		5.944 m.	Base del rodado total de máquina		5.944 m.
,, Rigid.		9' 6"	,, fixé		2.896 m.	,, rigido de máquina	2.896 m.
,, Total		38' 5"	,, total		11.710 m.	,, total de máquina y	
Length over Buffers		48' 1"	Longeur totale avec buttoirs		14.046 m.	,, tender	11.710 m.
Height (rail to top of chimney)		11' 6"	Hauteur maximum		3.505 m.	Largo sobre paragolpes		14.046 m.
Width (over cab)		8' 1"	Largeur maximum		2.464 m.	Altura (entre riel y chimenea)		3.505 m.
Axleload		9·4 tons	Charge maxima par essieu		9.55 tonnes	Ancho (afuera casilla)		2.464 m.
Adhesive Weight		27·7 tons	Poids adhérent		28.14 tonnes	Peso por eje		9.55 tonnes
Weight of Engine (in working order)		37·5 tons	Poids de la Machine, en marche		38.1 tonnes	Peso adherente		28.14 tonnes
,, ,, Tender (in working order)		23·1 tons	,, du Tender, en marche		23.5 tonnes	Peso de máquina en servicio		38.1 tonnes
						Peso de tender en servicio		23.5 tonnes
,, Engine and Tender (in working order)		60·6 tons	de la Machine et du Tender en marche		61.6 tonnes	Peso de máquina y tender en servicio	61.6 tonnes	
Tractive Effort at 85% B.P.		18,460 lb.	Effort de Traction à 85% du timbre		8.373 kg.	Fuerza de tracción con 85% presión de caldera		8.373 kg.
,, at 75% B.P.		16,290 lb.	,, à 75% du timbre		7.390 kg.	Fuerza de tracción con 75% presión	
Boiler Pressure		188 lb./sq. in.	Timbre		13 kg./cm.²	de caldera		7.390 kg.
Heating Surface—			Surface de chauffe—			Presión de caldera		13 kg./cm.²
Tubes		913 sq. ft.	Tubes		84.82 m.²	Superficie de calefacción—	
Firebox		97·5 sq. ft.	Boîte à feu		9.06 m.²	Tubos		84.82 m.²
						Caja de fuego		9.06 m.²
Total evaporative		1,010·5 sq. ft.	Surface totale de vaporisation		93.88 m.²	Total evaporativa		93.88 m.²
Grate Area		17 sq. ft.	Surface de grille		1.56 m.²	Superficie del emparrillado		1.58 m.²
Fuel Capacity		130 cub. ft.	Capacité en combustible		3.88 m.²	Capacidad de carbón		3.88 m.²
Water Capacity		2,300 gal.	,, en eau		10.46 m.²	,, agua		10.46 m.²
Adhesive Factor (at 75% B.P.)		3·8	Coefficient d'adhérence (à 75% du timbre)		3.8	Factor de adhesión (con 75% presión de caldera)		3,8

| GAUGE 3' 6" | VOIE DE 1.067 M. | TROCHA 1.067 M. | 17 |

The Silverton Tramway was a private railway established in 1888 when the states of New South Wales and South Australia could not agree on which of them should operate a railway across the border. It ran for 35 miles from Broken Hill & Silverton in NSW to Cockburn in South Australia. Between 1912 and 1915, it took delivery of four 4-6-0 locomotives from Beyer Peacock, which were designated Class A. No. 21 is preserved at the National Railway Museum, Port Adelaide. (Alon Siton collection)

In the First World War, Robinson's Great Central Railway Class 8K 2-8-0 was chosen by the Railway Operating Division (ROD) for military use. No. 2004, built by the GCR, was the 350th ROD locomotive to go to France, and was one of thirteen bought from the War Department in the 1920s for the Richmond Vale Railway in Newcastle, New South Wales. She was the last in service, in 1973, and is one of three to survive in Australia, now cosmetically restored at Richmond Vale. (Jeff Mullier)

Central station is Sydney's third terminus, replacing the original 1855 station and another from the 1870s. These earlier facilities had become too small and were in any case too far from the business district. Work started in 1901 and it opened in 1906, with its landmark clock tower added in 1921. Reaching a height of almost 280 feet, it provided the photographer with this view south, in which at least seven steam locomotives were captured. (ETH Zürich)

This official portrait shows Midland Railway of Western Australia Class A 2-8-2 No. 21, the first of a series of nine built by Kitson from 1925. They were of similar outline to the Kitson 4-6-2s built for the same railway. Designed to combine light axle loading with the power to haul heavy freight trains, they lasted until ousted by diesels in the late 1950s. (Alon Siton collection)

1926 saw the arrival in South Australia of three classes of very American appearance. These were the 500 Class 4-8-2, 600 Class 4-6-2 and 700 Class 2-8-2. Ten of each were built by Armstrong Whitworth in Newcastle-upon-Tyne, and they revolutionised operations, eliminating costly double-heading. The 500s were designed for heavy passenger duties and fast freights over the Adelaide Hills. Rear boosters were added in 1929, making them 4-8-4s, and several received stylish valances along the running plate. No. 504 *Tom Barr Smith* is preserved in the railway museum at Port Adelaide. (Tony Haynes)

Series of Locomotives for Queensland being shipped on the " Belray."
4-8-0 LOCOMOTIVES FOR THE QUEENSLAND GOVERNMENT RAILWAYS. *(See opposite page.)*
Built by Sir W. G. Armstrong, Whitworth & Co. Ltd.

At this time, Armstrong Whitworth's giant Scotswood Works by the Tyne was a busy place, for in 1927 the firm turned out a batch of twenty-five Class C17 4-8-0s for the Queensland Government Railways. Here they await loading onto the *Belray* for their long voyage to Pinkenba Wharf in Brisbane. This vessel was launched the previous year from one of Armstrong Whitworth's slipways. We will encounter her again later. Four of these handsome 4-8-0s are preserved. (Alon Siton collection)

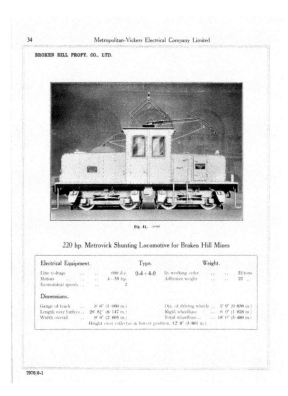

In 1928, Metropolitan Vickers supplied three 3-foot-6-inch-gauge electric locomotives to the Broken Hill Proprietary Co. Ltd, as seen here in the manufacturer's catalogue. They were joined by a fourth from England then another four built locally. They worked at two South Australia ironstone quarries, and one of the locomotives is preserved at the National Railway Museum in Port Adelaide. (Alon Siton collection)

In 1948, the Tasmanian Government Railways took delivery of the first of eight 204-hp Drewry diesel-mechanical shunters from Vulcan Foundry. They were a versatile design manufactured with inside or outside frames to suit different gauges. Vulcan built similar locos for Algeria, New Zealand, Portugal, South Africa, Tanganyika, Norway, Queensland and British Guyana, as well as for British Railways. This is No. V8 at Burnie on New Year's Day in 1973. (Melanie Dennis)

This very handsome locomotive is Western Australian Government Railways PM Class 4-6-2 No. 713, built by North British in Glasgow in 1949. The PMs were intended as an improved version of the PR-class passenger engines, themselves a development of the North British-built P Class of the 1920s. They were, however, rough riders and were instead deployed on goods trains. Several survive in preservation. (Alon Siton collection)

Australia's close ties with Britain meant that locomotives continued to be exported in quantity until the 1950s. In fact, the order books at Beyer Peacock were so full, construction of twenty of these large 4-8-2+2-8-4 Beyer Garratts for Queensland was subcontracted to Société Franco Belge in Raismes, France. No. 1002, seen here, was the second of the original batch of ten built in Manchester in 1950. You can see how far the Garratt had evolved from the little Tasmanian engine of 1909. (Alon Siton collection)

Another British-built locomotive of 1950 bound for Australia was 4-6-2 no.1011, seen here awaiting shipment from Birkenhead Docks. She was the first of Queensland Government Railways' BB18¼ Class, built at Vulcan Foundry and totalling 35 locomotives. A further twenty were ordered from Queensland firm Walkers Ltd, but shortages of staff and materials slowed delivery and the very last, no.1089, didn't enter service until 1958, becoming Australia's last new steam locomotive. (Alon Siton collection)

Tasmanian Government Railways' X Class was a 600hp Bo-Bo designed and powered by English Electric, the first main-line diesel-electric locos in Australia. Driver Stan Merry is in charge of nos.X4 and X5 on a test run at Western Junction soon after delivery from the UK in late 1950. X1-20 were built at Vulcan Foundry with another twelve coming from EE Preston. Like most EE diesels, they were reliable machines and lasted until the late 1980s. (Melanie Dennis)

This rakish-looking 4-8-2 was Western Australia Government Railways' Class W No. 923, built by Beyer Peacock in 1951. Sixty were ordered for the territory's lightly laid network, replacing an assortment of worn-out locomotives. With their 10-ton axle loading, roller bearings, compensated springs, a self-cleaning smokebox, self-emptying ashpan, thermic syphons and steam reversing gear, they really were state-of-the-art machines. Several are preserved. (Alon Siton collection)

The aforementioned Silverton Tramway saw WAGR's W Class as an ideal design for their needs and ordered four for themselves. They differed in appearance from their western counterparts, with their stylish boiler cowling. The drab, wet streets of post-war Lancashire could not provide more of a contrast to the antipodean destination of No. W22 *Justin Hancock*, seen here on her way to Birkenhead in 1951. (Alon Siton collection)

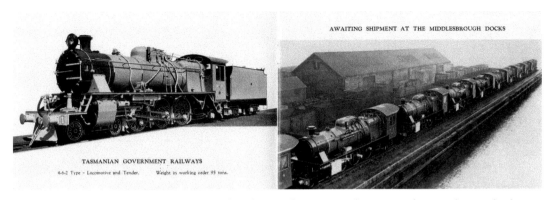

In 1937 Robert Stephenson's merged with Hawthorn's, so when its Darlington factory built the ten Class M Pacifics for Tasmania in 1951, their works plates carried the name 'Robert Stephenson & Hawthorn'. Note the mixed-gauge rails on which the entire class stands, awaiting shipment from Middlesbrough docks. (Alon Siton collection)

Here is No. M5, one of the ten Tasmanian 4-6-2s, in storage at Hobart in 1973. Having been withdrawn in 1971, she was awaiting movement to the Glenorchy site of the fledgling Tasmanian Transport Museum. M2 was repatriated and is a rusting hulk at the Tanfield Railway, just 36 miles from her Darlington birthplace. There is little prospect of her being steamed, but she is a poignant reminder of the role played by British firms in exporting locomotives to the world. Happily, all of her sisters survive in Australia. (Melanie Dennis)

This spectacular photograph taken from a Clydeside crane in 1951 shows North British-built Victorian Railways Class R 4-6-4 No. R701 and a sister on board the *Dunedin Star*, built on the Clyde a year earlier. The class of seventy locomotives had 6-foot-1-inch coupled wheels for express passenger duties, and possessed a good turn of speed, but were soon replaced by diesel and electric traction. (Alon Siton collection)

A closer look at one of the Class R 4-6-4s, No. R703. Sister locomotive R704 was displayed at the 1951 Festival of Britain on London's South Bank, and she is one of seven that survive in preservation. Notice the stylish semi-streamlined valances over the wheels, and the German-style smoke deflectors, similar to those fitted to Gresley's LNER A3 Pacifics in BR days. (Alon Siton collection)

They don't come much bigger than this. New South Wales Government Railways Beyer Garratt No. 6003 was one of the forty-seven members of the AD60 Class 4-8-4+4-8-4, built at Beyer Peacock in Manchester in 1952. Like all Garratts, she consists of a large boiler articulated between two locomotive units, and by all accounts the AD60s gave excellent service. Four of these giants are preserved, including No. 6029, which has been restored to working order. (Alon Siton collection)

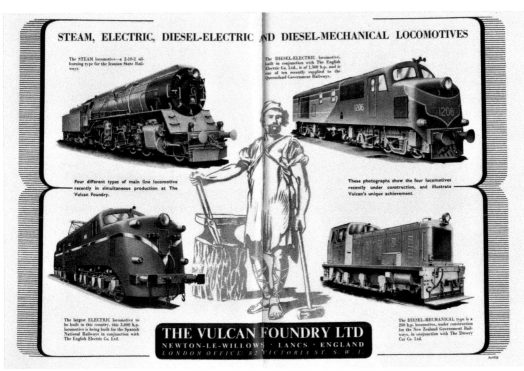

This advertisement of 1953 was designed to illustrate the versatility of Vulcan Foundry and English Electric. It features, anti-clockwise from top left, a 2-10-2 steam locomotive for Iran; the largest electric locomotive (at that time) to be built in Britain, destined for Spain; a Drewry diesel-mechanical shunter for New Zealand; and a stylish 1,500-hp diesel-electric for Queensland. (Alon Siton collection)

Here is another of Queensland's English Electric diesels, which shares many aesthetic features with the later Napier *Deltic* prototype, trialled successfully on British Railways. QGR's 1200 Class was ordered in 1951 and operated the 'Sunlander', a long-distance passenger service from Brisbane to Cairns, inaugurated in 1953. The route rather incongruously included a stretch along Denison Street in Rockhampton, as seen here. (Alon Siton collection)

Another Beyer Peacock order subcontracted to Societe Franco-Belge was for a class of ten 3-foot-6-inch-gauge 4-8-2+2-8-4 Garratts for South Australian Railways. They hauled heavy mineral trains on the Broken Hill line. Two are preserved: No. 402 at the Zig Zag Railway, Lithgow and No. 409 at the National Railway Museum in Port Adelaide. This official works portrait shows No. 405, built in 1953. (Alon Siton collection)

More German-style smoke deflectors on display at Gladstone Dock in Liverpool in 1954 on new J Class 2-8-0s bound for Victorian Railways. Nearest the camera are J547 and 548, part of a Vulcan Foundry order for sixty, the last steam locomotives ordered for Victoria. Note the fuel-oil reservoirs on the tenders, as fitted to the later members of the class. The unusually high boiler was to permit possible conversion from broad to standard gauge. Eleven examples are preserved. (Alon Siton collection)

Among the more unusual British-built diesel locomotive types to be exported were the X Class 2-Do-2 diesel-electrics of 1954. They were a joint venture between Beyer Peacock and Metropolitan-Vickers in Stockton-on-Tees for the Western Australia Government Railway. Sharing the same unreliable Crossley engine as British Railways' Metro-Vick Co-Bos, they lasted far longer than their BR cousins, thanks to the engineering knowhow of their Australian fitters. No. 1001 *Yalagonga* was the first of forty-eight built. They were withdrawn by 1988, and six are preserved including No. 1001. (Alon Siton collection)

The Commonwealth Railways crossed Australia from Kalgoorlie in the west to Port Pirie in the south and included the line that ran north to Alice Springs. A separate section ran south from Darwin to Birdum in the Northern Territory. Much of the CR's network passed through inhospitable desert, and in 1952 fourteen Sulzer-powered diesel-electrics, known as NSU Class, were ordered from Birmingham Carriage & Wagon. They entered service in 1954 and were highly successful. Preserved NSU52 rumbles toward Quorn with a mixed train on the Pichi Richi Railway in 2019. (Steve Burrows)

The twenty-four locomotives of Western Australian Government Railways' Class V 2-8-2 were built by Robert Stephenson & Hawthorn under subcontract from Beyer-Peacock. They performed well but, as with so many perfectly good steam locomotives around the world, their working lives were cut short by the onset of dieselisation. This is No. 1209, built in Darlington in 1955 and photographed on a freight train at Wagin. (Alon Siton collection)

We now hop across the Tasman Sea to New Zealand. Scottish engineer Robert Fairlie patented his double-ended articulated locomotive with all wheels powered in 1864. 0-4-4-0T *Josephine* was one of a pair of 'Double Fairlies' built by Vulcan Foundry in 1872 for the 3-foot-6-inch-gauge Dunedin to Port Chalmers Railway. Happily, she is preserved in the Otago Settlers Museum where she is seen in 2015. (Bernard Spragg)

Twelve of these little Class A 0-4-0T locomotives were built in 1873 by Dübs in Glasgow, and they served New Zealand well on branch-line and shunting duties. They were later put to good use by industrial railways, notably hauling loaded trains on the difficult 50-mile Taupo Totara Timber Company railway, with its 1 in 30 gradients and tight curves. Four are preserved, including A62 seen here at the Packard Motor Museum in Maungatapere. (Glen Satherley)

No. 508 was one of ten Class L 2-4-0Ts built by Avonside of Bristol for New Zealand Railways in 1877. Later sold to the Public Works Department and again to Portland Cement in Whangarei, she was in use until 1964. In 1974, she was purchased by the Tauranga Historic Village, where she ran for another fourteen years until the museum closed. She was then purchased by Shantytown Heritage Park and after overhaul returned to work in 2002, her 125th year. Two of her sisters also survive in preservation. (Bernard Spragg)

Another pretty little 2-4-0T for New Zealand, Neilson's of Glasgow supplied this 1878 example for the South Island, where she was a member of the D Class. Like her North Island counterpart above, she was sold into industrial service, in 1918, to the New Zealand Refrigerating Company. She served her new owners well, until retirement in the early 1970s, when she was placed on a plinth for posterity. In 1985, she was given to the Pleasant Point Museum and Railway & Historical Society on condition she was restored to working order. (Bernard Spragg)

Ferrymead Heritage Park, Christchurch, on New Zealand's South Island, is home to 'Kitty', one of only three Kitson steam tram locomotives in existence, and the only one in operating order. Eight were built in Leeds from 1880 and shipped to Christchurch for the Canterbury Tramway Company. Although superseded by electric trams, she was kept in working order for engineering work, and she remained the property of the Canterbury Transport Board until the 1960s. Unlike the Beyer Peacock steam tram engine for New South Wales, she has a horizontal boiler. (Bernard Spragg)

This sturdy 0-4-2T was one of two Class H locomotives built in 1886 by Neilson's of Glasgow for use on the Rimutaka Incline. They followed four earlier examples built by Avonside. Her frames conceal additional horizontal driving wheels, which gripped a central rail, using the patent Fell mountain railway system. In the early 1950s New Zealand Railways built a new tunnel, bypassing the incline and rendering the Class Hs redundant. One of the six locomotives is preserved. (ETH Zürich)

A more conventional product of Neilson's was this 0-6-0ST of 1888, locomotive No. 1 of the Kaihu Valley Railway. This remote line was built to carry timber to the town of Dargaville, near the northern extremity of New Zealand. No. 1 was one of the ubiquitous Class F locomotives, seen all over the country, and several are preserved. (ETH Zürich)

Perhaps learning from Australia's experience, and being a much smaller country, in 1870 New Zealand's government decreed that all of the nation's railways would be 3-foot-6-inch gauge. This vintage postcard shows the arrival of an express train at Palmerston North, on the North Island, in 1891. Note that the train is mixed, conveying both passengers and goods. (ETH Zürich)

This wonderful illustration by John Swain from a 1900 issue of *The Engineer* shows two much larger locomotives destined for New Zealand. They are a Ua Class passenger 4-6-0 and a B Class 4-8-0 goods engine. Several of each type were built by Sharp, Stewart of Glasgow and further examples were built locally. They were designed by locomotive superintendent T. F. Rotherham, who later moved from New Zealand to the West Australian Government Railways. (Alon Siton collection)

Built in 1906, Dunedin's Flemish Renaissance-style station is still one of the most prominent landmarks in the city centre. Architect George Troup used contrasting white Oamaru limestone and black basalt in its construction, and its appearance earned him the nickname of 'Gingerbread George'. The mosaic floor of the booking hall features over 700,000 Royal Doulton porcelain tiles. (ETH Zürich)

The Class Ab 4-6-2 mixed-traffic locomotives, most of which came from North British in Glasgow, were one of the most successful and efficient New Zealand locomotive types – 141 were built. O. S. Nock commented on their excellent design and how easily they attained 60 mph despite their small driving wheels. They were introduced in 1915, and the last was withdrawn in 1969. (ETH Zürich)

The name of Armstrong Whitworth crops up again in connection with this locomotive, not as her builder, but her purchaser. B10 is a 0-4-0ST built by Hudswell Clarke in Leeds in 1924 for Armstrong Whitworth, contractors for the Waihi to Tauranga section of the North Island East Coast Main Trunk Railway. The locomotive was then sold into industrial use before being rescued for preservation in 1989. She now hauls passenger trains on the harbourside at Oamaru Steam & Rail. (Bernard Spragg)

In less than twenty years, the Beyer Garratt locomotive evolved from the little Tasmanian machine to this magnificent double Pacific. This is one of three members of New Zealand Government Railways' G Class, built by Beyer Peacock in 1928. These large-wheeled six-cylinder 4-6-2+2-6-4s featured Gresley-type valve gear on their middle cylinders, and were so powerful they were known to break drawbars. (Alon Siton collection)

As well as the little steam tram engine seen earlier, the Tramway Historical Society at Ferrymead is custodian of one of these Class Ec electric locos, where she has been restored to working order. Six were built by English Electric in 1928 for the Christchurch-Lyttelton line, which opened in 1867. That route featured a 1.6-mile-long tunnel in which steam trains caused smoke to accumulate, so it was electrified in the 1920s. (Alon Siton collection)

North British built forty 3-foot-6-inch-gauge J Class 4-8-2s for New Zealand, from 1939 onwards. This view inside the works shows several under construction. The third locomotive from the camera has been fitted with her distinctive long boiler cowling, and her numberplate, reading No. 1201, can be discerned. (ETH Zürich)

This photograph shows the first of the Class Js, No. 1200 arriving on New Zealand's North Island. She is undergoing the specialised and labour-intensive business of unloading a 70-ton locomotive from the ship that has carried her half way around the world. Note the lifting beam, which appears to be North British property. (Alon Siton collection)

During the Second World War, New Zealand Railways needed something more economical than steam power for light passenger duties. Ten diesel railcars were ordered from Vulcan Foundry, of which one was lost en route in a German U-boat attack. Powered by a six-cylinder 250-hp Frichs engine, in October 1940 RM50 set the New Zealand Railways speed record of 78 mph, which still stands. She is preserved for posterity at Ashburton. (Bernard Spragg)

New Zealand's Ja Class 4-8-2 was a development of the earlier J, and although the first series was built locally, the last sixteen, like the original J Class, were supplied by North British. This 1952 official works portrait shows no.1287 prior to shipping from the Clyde. They were the last steam locomotives built for New Zealand Railways, and lasted in service until 1971. (ETH Zürich)

No. 1806 was one of seven Ew Class electric Bo+Bo+Bo articulated locomotives built in 1952 for New Zealand Railways by Robert Stephenson & Hawthorn in association with English Electric. They operated passenger and freight services on the electrified network around Wellington until 1988, and two survive in preservation. (Roger Norfolk)

Another preservation group based at Ferrymead is New Zealand's Diesel Traction Group, guardians of the sole surviving English Electric Df Class 2Co-Co2 locomotive. Introduced in 1954, the 1,500-hp locomotives were the country's first main-line diesel-electrics, intended for heavy goods work on the North Island. Of thirty-one units ordered from English Electric, only ten were built, NZR preferring the later Dg Class. This photo shows now-preserved No. 1501 when new. (Melanie Dennis)

The aforementioned Dg Class, built by English Electric at Vulcan Foundry from 1955 totalled forty-two locomotives. The 750-hp locos had an A1A-A1A wheel arrangement and were far more versatile than the much larger Dfs. Preserved No. 772 is main-line certificated, and is seen here with an excursion train crossing the Mataura River at Gore in tandem with Di Class No. 1102, built at EE's Queensland offshoot in the 1960s. No. 772 is owned by the Diesel Traction Group and resides at Ferrymead. (Andrew Surgenor)

Fiji was one of the few Pacific islands with railways. In 1912, Hudswell Clarke of Leeds built the first of thirty short-wheelbase 0-6-0s for Colonial Sugar Refining. This official workshop portrait shows *Sigatoka,* named in honour of the extension of the Rarawai-Kavanangasau Light Railway to the town of that name. Having been converted to diesel power for use on a Fijian tourist railway she is now restored to steam at the Statfold Barn Railway in England, where she is named *Fiji*. (Alon Siton collection)

By far the largest territory in the British Empire was Canada, whose first railway locomotive, like that of so many nations, was built at the works of Robert Stephenson in Newcastle-upon-Tyne. This was the *Dorchester,* built in 1836 for the Champlain and St Lawrence Railroad. At least two different replicas of this engine were built for the Canadian railway centenary. Curiously, one was an 0-4-0, and this half-scale version a 2-4-0. (ETH Zürich)

Canada's Grand Trunk Railway was formed in London in 1852 and eventually covered Quebec, Ontario, Michigan and New England. This 4-4-0 was built in 1859 and was the first locomotive to emerge from the railway's own workshops in Montreal. Appropriately for a British company, No. 209 was named *Trevithick* after the Cornish father of the steam locomotive. (ETH Zürich)

This page from a publication by North British of Glasgow provides us with an interesting comparison between the classic American 4-4-0, still being built in the UK, and the typical contemporary British machine of the same wheel arrangement. We have an 1871-built locomotive, another for the Grand Trunk Railway, and a Caledonian Railway 4-4-0 of 1876. (Alon Siton collection)

Following the completion of the United States of America's transcontinental railroad in 1869, the same feat was achieved in Canada in 1885. This was the year that the Canadian Pacific Railway first connected Vancouver on the west coast to Montreal in Quebec. The line through British Columbia's Fraser Canyon was completed in the 1880s. (ETH Zürich)

AMERICAN MOGUL LOCOMOTIVE. NEWFOUNDLAND RAILWAY.
Mʳ JAMES CLEMINSON M.INST.CE., WESTMINSTER, ENGINEER.

From Canada's western canyons we cross to one of her easternmost provinces, where the Newfoundland Railway was the recipient of this 2-6-0. Named *St Johns,* she was designed by James Cleminson and built by R&W Hawthorn in Newcastle-upon-Tyne in 1882. Her bar frames, large wooden cab, spark-arresting chimney and cowcatcher contribute to her typically American appearance. (Alon Siton collection)

Preserved on the Prairie Dog Central Railway, at Inkster Junction near Winnipeg, Manitoba, is another example of an 1882 UK-built American type, but of the more usual 4-4-0 wheel arrangement. She was built by Dübs of Glasgow for the Canadian Pacific Railway, becoming their No. 22. Later to become No. 3, she is the oldest operating locomotive in Canada. (Michael Berry)

Newcastle-upon-Tyne's Jubilee Exhibition of 1887 marked the fiftieth year of Victoria's reign, and was an opportunity for Tyneside's manufacturers to show off their wares. Among the exhibits was this unusual narrow-gauge, outside-framed 2-6-2 built by Hawthorn's for the Canadian Harbour Grace Railway in Newfoundland, as illustrated by John Swain in *The Engineer*. Named *Emigrant*, she and her sister were initially ordered for Western Australia's Midland Railway, but lack of finance meant she went to Canada instead. (Alon Siton collection)

Rising above Place du Canada, Montreal's iconic Windsor station was once the hub of Canada's east to west railway system. Opened by the Canadian Pacific Railway in 1889, it is one of the nation's most striking examples of Romanesque Revival architecture. The station was enlarged several times, and in this early twentieth-century view the building of the main tower is in progress as passengers await their train. Most of the buildings survive but trains no longer call here. (ETH Zürich)

By the time Canadian National Railways was formed in 1918, the rail companies of North America were largely self-sufficient, so the importing of locomotives from Britain had ceased. The station at the British Columbian outpost of Kamloops did not open until 1927. This is now one of the stops on the famous Rocky Mountaineer tourist route. (ETH Zürich)

The first Union station in Canada's largest city, Toronto, opened in 1872. It was replaced in 1927 by this beaux arts masterpiece in the heart of the city, which unlike its Montreal counterpart, is still very much in use, serving 250,000 passengers daily. The station was opened by Edward, Prince of Wales, and is linked by a subterranean passageway to the opulent Royal York Hotel, across the street. (Colin Alexander)

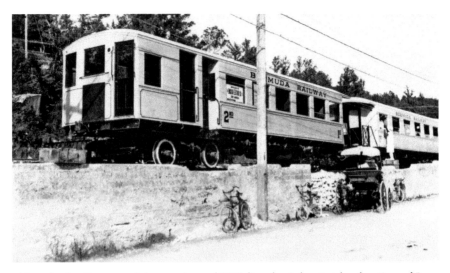

Several hundred miles east of the continental USA lies the Atlantic island nation of Bermuda. Its railway was a small operation. Motive power consisted of British-built railcars with Drewry mechanicals and Cravens bodies, assembled by English Electric in Preston. They could be coupled together and controlled in multiple, and augmented with trailer cars. When the line closed much of its stock, including the railcars, was sold for use in British Guyana. (Colin Churcher)

Heading south-west to the Caribbean now, this dramatic shot portrays some very trusting railway workers posing for the camera. It shows a Jamaica Government Railway steam crane suspending a locomotive in mid-air. The crane was built by Cowans Sheldon in Carlisle in 1922, and 0-6-0T No. 7 by Kitson's of Leeds in 1879. In the background, symbolising the growing American influence in the global locomotive export market is a Baldwin-built 2-8-2. (Alon Siton collection)

Cambridge station, seen here in 1970, was in Jamaica's St James parish, and was on the route from Kingston to Montego Bay. Built around 1894 in a unique Jamaican/Georgian style, it was a two-storey timber structure with a zinc roof. The island's passenger service ended in 1992, but a limited amount of freight continues on Jamaica's remaining rail network, carrying bauxite and sugar cane for export. (Nick Booker)

JAMAICA GOVERNMENT RAILWAY.

TYPE ... **4.8.0.**   GAUGE ... **4 FT. 8½ IN. = 1435·1 M/M.**

ENGINE.

CYLINDERS:—Diameter	19½ in.	= 495·3 m/m
Stroke	24 in.	= 609·6 m/m
HEATING SURFACE:—Tubes	... 1285 sq. ft.	= 119·3 M²
Firebox	... 127 ,,	= 11·8 M².
Total	1412 ,,	= 131·1 M².
FIREGRATE AREA	24·25 ,,	= 2·26 M².
WORKING PRESSURE	... 180 lbs. per sq. in.	= 12·65 Kilos per c/m².
WHEELS:—Coupled, Diameter	... 3 ft. 10 in.	= 1168·4 m/m.
Front, ,, ...	... 2 ft. 6 in.	= 762 m/m.
WHEEL-BASE:—Rigid	... 8 ft. 3 in.	= 2514·6 m/m.
Total	... 23 ft. 0 in.	= 7010·4 m/m.
Engine and Tender	46 ft. 10½ in.	= 14287·5 m/m.
WEIGHT:—In Working Order	... 53·4 tons	= 54257 Kilos.
On Coupled Wheels	... 41·65 tons	= 43184 Kilos.

In 1901, Kitson's built a trio of 4-8-0 locomotives for the Jamaica Government Railway. The island's network had then recently been extended to serve an American military base at Vernamfield, Clarendon and traffic increased accordingly. The 4-8-0 found favour in Jamaica, for eleven more locomotives of that wheel arrangement would follow from various manufacturers. (Alon Siton collection)

JAMAICA GOVERNMENT RAILWAYS.

TYPE ... 0.6.6.0.   GAUGE ... 4 FT. 8½ IN. = 1435·1 M/M.

"KITSON-MEYER" ENGINE.

4 CYLINDERS:—Diameter...	13 in.	= 330·2 m/m.
Stroke ...	22 in.	= 558·8 m/m.
HEATING SURFACE:—Tubes	1328 sq. ft.	= 123·3 M².
Firebox	130 ,,	= 12·1 M².
Total ...	1458 ,,	= 135·4 M².
FIREGRATE AREA ...	26 ,,	= 2·4 M².
WORKING PRESSURE	180 lbs. per sq. in.	= 12·65 Kilos per c/m².
WHEELS:—Coupled, Diameter	3 ft. 6 in.	= 1066·8 m/m.
WHEEL-BASE:—Rigid ...	7 ft. 9 in.	= 2362·2 m/m.
Total ...	29 ft. 9 in.	= 9067·7 m/m.
WEIGHT:—In Working Order	80·75 tons	= 82045 Kilos.
On Coupled Wheels ...	80·75 tons	= 82045 Kilos.
TANK CAPACITY ...	2,500 gallons	= 11358 litres.
FUEL CAPACITY ...	4 tons coal	= 4·06 tonnes.
TRACTIVE FORCE AT 75% OF BOILER PRESSURE ...	23895 lbs.	= 10839 Kilos.

The same Leeds manufacturer supplied Jamaica with a trio of these Kitson Meyer 0-6-6-0T locomotives in 1904. Theoretically a very powerful design, with all six axles driven, they proved uneconomical in service. Nevertheless, the Kitson Meyer was one of the most satisfactory essays in steam locomotive articulation until the advent of the Beyer Garratt. (Alon Siton collection)

Jamaica was another overseas recipient of diesel-electric locomotives from English Electric, with a class of twelve 750-hp units arriving from 1955, such as No. 87 seen here. They were similar to other EE diesels for Australia, Nigeria and the former Gold Coast. (Alon Siton collection)

Taken in 1963 from the cab of one of the EE diesels, this photo looks back along a mixed train as it negotiates the mountainous section between Kingston and Montego Bay. This was the island's main line, over 110 miles long and cut through solid rock in places. It connected the two largest cities and visited most of the island's other major towns en route. (Alon Siton collection)

In 1963, these Metropolitan Cammell diesel railcars were the latest thing on Jamaican railways. This one has arrived at Kingston from Montego Bay. There has been much discussion about reinstating passenger services on Jamaica to reduce congestion on the roads as much of the rail infrastructure remains intact. (Alon Siton collection)

St Kitts' 2-foot-6-inch-gauge sugar cane railway once circled the whole island. Six 0-4-2ST locomotives were imported from Kerr Stuart in Stoke-on-Trent, and even though the last of them was replaced by diesel traction by 1972, one steam engine survives and may be restored. After the sugar traffic ceased, part of the railway reopened as a tourist attraction, combining with a bus to provide a circular tour of the island for tourists, often in conjunction with cruise ships. (John Oram)

As well as the 0-4-2STs for St Kitts, Kerr Stuart supplied narrow-gauge 0-6-2T locomotives to various customers, including the Gunthorpe's Estate Railway of Antigua. Kerr Stuart No. 4404 of 1927 was given the name *Joan*, and she is now restored to working order, as seen here in Wales at Llanfair Caereinion on the Welshpool & Llanfair Railway, in May 2016. (Thomas Walker mkttransportmedia.smugmug.com)

This rare postcard view shows the short-lived railway hugging the coast at Bathsheba on the east coast of Barbados. The railway had recruited its general manager, Mr Grundy, from the Great Western Railway, but he died of yellow fever before the opening, and his son took his place. Originally 3-foot-6-inch gauge, the railway eventually extended to 21½ miles and was relaid in 1898 to the narrower gauge of 2 feet 6 inches. An early economic casualty, the railway closed in 1937. The Atlantis Hotel survives today. (ETH Zürich)

Kitson's built seventeen of these handsome 4-4-0T locomotives for the Trinidad Government Railway, where they were joined by another from Nasmyth Wilson. Built between 1897 and 1907, they were the mainstay of the TGR main line until the arrival of more modern tender locomotives between the wars. (Alon Siton collection)

No.18 *Picton* was one of three 2-6-2T locomotives built by Hunslet in Leeds in 1927 for Sainte Madeleine Sugar Company in the south of Trinidad. She returned to England in 2002 and is the subject of a conservation project at the wonderful Middleton Railway, a mile from where she was built, as seen here in 2020. (Colin Alexander)

Trinidad Government Railway engine No. 32 was one of the locomotives that replaced the Kitson 4-4-0Ts. She is seen here in charge of a mixed train at Port of Spain, where the station still exists as a bus terminal. No. 32 was one of a pair of lightweight 4-6-0s built by Armstrong Whitworth in Newcastle-upon-Tyne in 1928. Most of the other 'new' locomotives on the island came from Canada's Montreal Locomotive Works. (Colin Churcher)

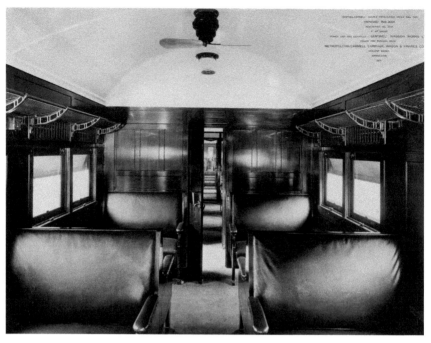

Trinidad was one of the many export destinations of the Sentinel steam railcar. This is a rare interior view of a double-articulated unit built in 1931. As usual it was a marriage of Metropolitan Cammell coachwork on a geared Sentinel chassis. Much later, some Wickham diesel multiple unit cars were sold by British Railways to Trinidad. (ETH Zürich)

Across the Columbus Channel from Trinidad lies Venezuela, whose eastern neighbour was formerly known as British Guyana. It seems odd that anyone would want to send a postcard like this, but it shows the aftermath of a collision on the Demerara Railway in 1895. The line had been surveyed by British civil engineer Frederick Catherwood, and it expanded slowly, carrying sugar cane and timber as well as significant passenger traffic. (ETH Zürich)

No. 31 *Sir Graeme* was one of two 4-6-4T locomotives built for British Guyana in 1924 by Hunslet of Leeds. They were joined by another two in 1947, and all were converted to oil-firing by 1952. The buffers could be folded back on the running plate, so there was no obstacle to any stray animal being cleared by the cowcatcher. (Alon Siton collection)

If this railcar in British Guyana looks familiar, it is because we saw one of them earlier in Bermuda. Built in 1931 by English Electric, they were powered by a Parsons petrol engine, and were sold by the Bermuda Government Railway to British Guyana in 1948, along with most of the other redundant railway equipment from the Atlantic island. (Colin Churcher)

This charming scene from British Guyana shows a locomotive purported to have been built in 1936. In truth, 0-6-0ST No. 33 *Sir Geoffry* is likely to have been assembled in that year using a new frame and other components from England, along with parts from scrapped No. 4 *Alexandra*, built by Sharp Stewart in Glasgow in 1863. This would explain her archaic appearance. (Colin Churcher)

It was common practice for British manufacturers to export rolling stock underframes for bodywork to be constructed locally. One such example is this coach chassis bound for British Guyana, built in 1957 by Gloucester Railway Carriage & Wagon. By the 1960s most freight traffic was lost to road transport, and Guyana's independent government saw the railway as a colonial relic. Despite carrying more than 2 million passengers annually, it closed in 1972. (Alon Siton collection)

Symbolising both the geographical edge of the Empire and the chronological end of the Empire, we reach the lonely Atlantic outpost of South Georgia, several hundred miles east of Tierra del Fuego. The southern elephant seals are oblivious to the German-built Krauss locomotive, a relic of the railway constructed by the British at Ocean Harbour, formerly New Fortuna Bay, to serve the whaling industry. It is thought that the loco has been lying there since she was overturned in the 1920s to permit removal of the rails. (Lex van Groningen)

Having travelled the Empire across three books, we turn to the astonishing variety of other countries supplied by Britain. Only fifty-five years after the Declaration of Independence, the USA turned to her former enemy for motive power. The Camden & Amboy Railroad in New Jersey took delivery of No. 1 *John Bull*, an 0-4-0 built by Robert Stephenson in Newcastle-upon-Tyne in 1831. On arrival she was assembled by Isaac Dripps, a young steamboat mechanic who added the front pony-truck to guide the locomotive around curves, an innovation that was adopted globally. In 1981 she was steamed by the Smithsonian Institute, at the age of 150 years. (Alon Siton collection)

Another Stephenson product was *Adler*, a Patentee type 2-2-2 built for the opening of the railway from Nuremberg to Fürth in 1835. At that time there was no capability in Germany to construct a functioning locomotive, so Robert Stephenson supplied *Adler* and two carriages, along with engineer William Wilson. The locomotive was shipped from the Tyne to Rotterdam in 'knocked-down' form, then by horse-drawn cart to Nuremberg where Wilson supervised her reassembly. He drove on her maiden journey before taking responsibility for instructing the railway's permanent drivers. (ETH Zürich)

For a fifty-year period starting in the 1830s, the railways of Russia were major customers of British locomotive builders. The engines were equipped for severe Russian winters: with enclosed cabs, frost-proof injectors and insulated pipework to prevent the freezing of lubricating oil. This is 2-4-0 No. 1578 of the Tambov-Saratov Railway, built by Kitson's of Leeds in 1869, complete with outsize spark-arresting chimney. (Julian Rainbow)

For a time, Stephenson's Forth Street works in Newcastle-upon-Tyne was the only locomotive factory in the world, but as railway mania spread other companies were established across Britain's industrial centres. One that sprang up across the Tyne in Gateshead was the firm of Black, Hawthorn, who in 1875 built four of these neat 0-6-0T engines for the Porto, Póvoa & Familicão Railway in Portugal. One is preserved in a museum in Lousado. (Alon Siton collection)

As railways evolved in different countries, some developed their own locomotive aesthetic, in the same way as their vernacular architecture. One such was France. Although built on the Clyde in 1882 by Neilson's, this 2-4-0 for the Chemins de fer du Midi is indisputably Gallic in outline. No. 93 was one of a batch of twenty, along with another twenty for the Chemins de fer de l'Ouest. (Alon Siton collection)

Another 1882-built Glaswegian 2-4-0, but destined for the other side of the world, was this pretty example built by Sharp Stewart for the Dutch-owned Java Staatsspoorwegen in Indonesia. As late as the 1970s they were still in service at Madiun in the east of Java for working the branch line to Ponorogo and Slahung, where No. B5007 was photographed in 1971. Sister engine B5004 is preserved at Taman Mini near Jakarta. (Alon Siton collection)

Meanwhile south of the Anglo-Scottish border, Kitson's was working on an order for the Imperial Government Railways of Japan. Yes, we used to export to Japan! 0-6-0T No. 40 was built in Leeds in 1882 and is now on display in Kyoto's railway museum. Japanese railways operated twenty-seven locomotives built by Kitson, along with 240 from North British, twenty-three from Vulcan Foundry, 138 from Nasmyth Wilson and 194 from Beyer Peacock. (Joe Hsu)

With more than a passing resemblance to some of the fantastic creations of Mr Rowland Emett, this 2-4-2T was an 1883 product of Dübs, Glasgow. Carrying the name *Gmo H Ross: Havana,* after William (Guillermo) H. Ross, a Scottish agent for Cuban sugar plantations. Her outsized cab and boiler mountings seem totally out of proportion compared to her tiny wheels. Dübs built two similar locomotives, albeit with larger wheels, for Queensland Government Railways. (Alon Siton collection)

Continuing the Latin American theme, locomotives built for the steeply graded metre-gauge Ferrocarril Antofagasta Bolivia had to cope with crossing the Andes, reaching an altitude of over 12,000 feet. In 1888, Robert Stephenson's of Newcastle-upon-Tyne built this little 4-6-0 for the railway, No. 27, named *Ascotan* after a region on the Bolivian border with Chile. Note the uneven wheel spacing to accommodate her deep firebox. (Alon Siton collection)

Not quite as mountainous as the Antofagasta, the 3-foot-gauge Ferrocarril La Guairá y Caracas linked the Venezuelan capital with the coast, on gradients as steep as 1 in 25. Beyer Peacock supplied four 0-6-2Ts in 1888, and one is seen here on the tortuous route. After forty-one years of service each of these locomotives was said to have accumulated a million kilometres. The line was electrified in the 1920s, but inevitably competition from road traffic led to closure in 1951. (Alon Siton collection)

Another splendid official works portrait showing a Neilson 2-6-0 of 1889, for the Compania de Ferrocarriles de Lorca a Baza y Aguilas (Great Southern of Spain Railway). She was given the number 1 and the name *Murcia*. Others of the same type were built by Kitson's and Sharp Stewart, and later North British. Totalling twenty-five engines, they were employed on iron ore trains to the port of Hornillo and were held in high esteem, some giving more than eighty years of service. (ETH Zürich)

INTEROCEANIC AND MEXICAN EASTERN RAILWAYS.
Diameter of Cylinders, 16″. Stroke of Cylinders, 20″. Gauge, metre. Heating Surface, 1441 sq. ft. Grate Area, 18·75 sq. ft. Tractive Power, 21,889 lbs. Total Weight, 76 tons.

The grandly-titled Ferrocarril Interoceánico de México was a British private venture whose 3-foot-gauge main line linked Mexico City to Veracruz. Kerr Stuart, better known for its tank locomotives, was the contractor for five American-type bar-framed 2-8-0s, including No. 74 seen here – built in 1904. Note the plate in front of her chimney, for mounting a headlamp. (Alon Siton collection)

The Ferrocarril Central Uruguay of Montevideo was a London-registered railway company, and the most important in Uruguay. This handsome 2-6-0T was built in Manchester by Beyer Peacock in 1906. Its British owners laid more than 1,000 miles of railway route here, and a cricket club was founded in the capital city by its British and Uruguayan employees. (Alon Siton collection)

The British railway influence was perhaps stronger in Argentina than anywhere else outside of the Empire, and one of General Peron's most popular decrees was the nationalisation of the British-owned railway system in 1948. The Ferrocarril Buenos Aires al Pacífico was one of the four main 5-foot-6-inch-gauge companies established by the British. This is FCBAP 4-6-0 No. 1255, built by North British in 1907. (Alon Siton collection)

The railways of continental Europe were increasingly self-sufficient as the nineteenth century progressed, but sometimes it was necessary to turn to outside manufacturers to meet motive power demands. In 1910, Beyer Peacock built six of these Class 685 4-6-0s for the Staats Spoorwegen (Dutch State Railways). More came from Germany, and the Dutch firm Werkspoor. They lasted for decades, and their four cylinders made them equally suited to passenger or freight trains. (Alon Siton collection)

As in Argentina, British-owned railways were big business in Brazil, and the metre-gauge Leopoldina Railway extended to almost 2,000 miles. In 1914, Robert Stephenson built a pair of charming 2-8-0s for that company. In the 1970s, one of these was sold to Usina Santo Amaro, and she is seen here hauling sugar cane for the mill at Baixa Grande in 1985. She is now in the care of the Brazilian Association of Railroad Preservation at Cruzeiro, where it is hoped she will be restored to operational condition. (Alon Siton collection)

The Royal State Railways of Siam, which became Thailand in 1939, was the customer for a pair of these fine metre-gauge 2-8-2 locomotives built by Nasmyth Wilson in Manchester. This official portrait shows No. 311 of 1924. Ominously though for British industry, Siamese orders for larger batches of locomotives would go to Baldwin in the USA. (Alon Siton collection)

TCDD, the Turkish State Railway, inherited a class of six powerful 2-8-2s from the Ottoman Railway Company. They were built by Robert Stephenson's in 1929. The ORC was a British concern built to connect Aydin to Izmir, for the transport of minerals and agricultural produce. TCDD No. 46102, seen here, was formerly ORC No. 131. Sister engine No. 46103 is preserved at Çamlik. (Alon Siton collection)

It is surprising that even as late as 1935, British manufacturers were taking major orders from China. The largest single-unit locomotives ever built in Britain were the KF Class 4-8-4s for the Chinese National Railway. Sixteen of them emerged from Vulcan Foundry, of which one was eventually brought back to the National Railway Museum at York, a fitting tribute to Britain's reputation as locomotive builder to the world. (Alon Siton collection)

The culmination of the development of the Kitson Meyer type was probably this massive 2-8-8-2 design for the Ferrocarriles Nacionales (Colombian National Railways). No. 57 was one of two such locomotives subcontracted out by Kitson's to Robert Stephenson & Hawthorn of Darlington, and built there in 1935. This is appropriate, for 110 years earlier Robert Stephenson himself was working in Colombia, and there he encountered the father of the steam locomotive, Richard Trevithick. (Alon Siton collection)

One of the world's highest railways was the Ferrocarril Central, in Peru, reaching an altitude of over 15,800 feet at La Cima Pass in the Andes. The Andes Class of 2-8-0s were produced by Beyer Peacock from 1935 especially for this gruelling route, and more than fifty of these powerful locomotives were built. They were very American in appearance, with short boilers and air sanding gear and air brakes to cope with gradients as steep as 1 in 25. (Alon Siton collection)

We finish with two images that portray the scale of the export operation. This impressive Class 15B 4-8-0 was bound for the Ferrocarril del Sud (Buenos Aires Great Southern Railway). She was one of a class of thirty built by Vulcan Foundry in 1948, and is about to join a sister engine on the deck of a ship at Birkenhead for the long voyage across the Atlantic Ocean. (Alon Siton collection)

Illustrating the perilous nature of shipping locomotives overseas, and the skill of the men who loaded and navigated the ships, this is the *Belray* again, seen earlier on the Tyne with a shipment for Australia. Here she is on the Mersey, with the Liver Building as a backdrop. She is laden with Belgian locomotives for China, but perhaps the smaller tenders at her bow were loaded in Liverpool? It is surprising how small the vessel is in comparison to the locomotives, and especially in comparison to the huge ships that import locomotives for Britain's railways today. (Alon Siton collection)